my first aquarium

Betty the
betta
fish

D1707889

my first aquarium

Betty the
betta
fish

Thank you for your purchase!

This book was made for you with love by Hanna K. Fuchs - graphic designer and aquarium enthusiast, wholeheartly caring for the animal wellbeing.

If you enjoyed the book, please, leave a comment on Amazon

And check out the rest of the series!

1

I'm Betty

...Hi!

My name is Betty.

And I'm a...

BETTA FISH!

What's a betta fish?

Well...

Here!

Let me show you.

We came from Thailand in Asia.

And always liked cosiness!

We lived in shallow, warm waters.

Because of that, we have a special feature: the Labirynth.

fin

labirynth

tail

fins

It lets us breathe above the water surface! Cool, right?

In the past we had to fight for territory...

We also weren't as colorful!

And the right food...

can make us more colorful!

Some bettas are brave and strong!

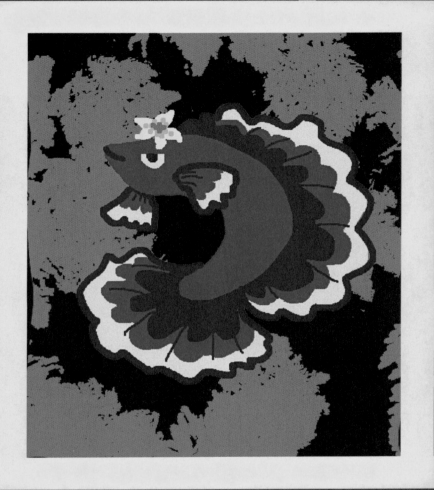

Some are known for their beauty.

And I... well.

I live in an Aquarium Shop!

Betta female

BETTA male

BETTA male

BETTA male

PLANTS $$

PLANTS $$$

And it's quite nice

in here...

...but also really crowded.

And that's why I decided

to find a new home.

2

New home

Ok... Let's get to it.

"Tanks for rent"…

Most offers are like this:

Tiny… and empty.

How sad!

And... imagine, that you

look through a glass jar.

It's fun for a while...

But not for your
WHOLE LIFE!

And that's how

living in the bowl feels.

BETTA TANK CUBE

VISIT NOW!

FOR RENT

Goodnight, Betty!

THE END

Made in the USA
Middletown, DE
28 August 2024